THE GOD OF VENGEANCE

Sholem Asch

Translated by
Richard Nelson
with
Robert Marx

BROADWAY PLAY PUBLISHING INC
New York
www.broadwayplaypub.com
info@broadwayplaypub.com

Cover photo: shtetl, Eastern Europe, 1916/1917

First edition: June 2019
I S B N: 978-0-88145-843-5

Book design: Marie Donovan
Page make-up: Adobe InDesign
Typeface: Palatino

INTRODUCTION
Robert Marx

Beyond the Pale—

BBC correspondent David Mazower (Sholem Asch's great-grandson) once summarized the production history of *The God of Vengeance* as "admired, translated, parodied, panned, banned, prosecuted, withdrawn, forgotten, revived, celebrated." Other plays have gone through similar cycles of abandonment and resurrection, but none with quite the political and social nightmares attached to Asch's most controversial drama.

Raised in the Russian-speaking zone of eastern Poland, Asch (1880-1957) was the youngest of ten children in a Hasidic family. Despite his strict religious upbringing in a community that disapproved of secular values, he learned German, read widely in European literature and found his way to Warsaw before he was twenty. There, he became part of Y L Peretz's Yiddish-language literary circle. His first short stories were published in 1900. *The God of Vengeance* was Asch's fourth play, written in 1906 and inspired by his seeing Rudolph Schildkraut perform Shylock in Max Reinhardt's production of *The Merchant of Venice* at Berlin's Deutsches Theater. Asch wrote *The God of Vengeance* with Schildkraut in mind.

Translated from Yiddish into German, the play premiered at the Deutsches Theater on March 19, 1907 and continued for six months (a substantial run at that time), playing in repertory with *The Government Inspector*, *Romeo and Juliet*, and Goethe's *The Siblings*. Asch's script was immediately acclaimed as a Yiddish counterpart to the 'problem plays' of Ibsen and Shaw, notably *Mrs Warren's Profession*. For Schildkraut, the anti-hero role of brothel owner Yekel Tchaftchovitch was a personal triumph, and he continued to play the part in German, Yiddish and English language productions for the next twenty years.

The God of Vengeance soon became the first Yiddish drama to be widely translated and staged throughout Europe. Later in 1907, its second production took place in St. Petersburg, followed by an American premiere in New York, performed in its original Yiddish, with David Kessler (a major star of the day) as Tschaftchovitch. Translations appeared in Polish, Hebrew, English, Italian, French, Dutch, Czech, Swedish and Norwegian. A Russian silent-film version (now lost) was made in 1912.

Notoriety was a key part of *The God of Vengeance*'s international success. Nearly every production sparked some level of critical controversy due to the play's conflicting themes of hypocrisy and religious faith, rebellion and tradition, its brothel setting, graphic domestic violence, "gutter poetry" reminiscent of Wedekind, and an unprecedented, erotic scene of lesbian seduction. (Along with notoriety came parody. The success of *The God of Vengeance* was so fast and widespread that in 1908, Yiddish essayist and translator Dovid Frishman wrote *The God of Mercy*—in which gay male references satirized Asch's lesbian scenes.)

The initial American response was typical, with New York's Yiddish-language press sharply divided about Kessler's 1907 production. The liberal (and secular) *Jewish Daily Forward* praised the play as a deeply moral poetic drama, while the orthodox *Morning Journal* condemned it as a depraved defamation of Jewish character.

Controversy attracted audiences. Everywhere, *The God of Vengeance* was a hit. Into the 1930s, actor-manager Maurice Schwartz kept the play in his Yiddish Art Theatre repertory on Second Avenue in New York, with Stella Adler as one of the prostitutes. (She would soon move uptown as a founding member of the Group Theatre on Broadway.) The peerless Russian-Yiddish actor Solomon Mikhoels played Tschaftchovitch in Moscow revivals. In 1930, the legendary Berlin UFA film studio announced that Alexis Granowsky, a founder of GOSNET (the Moscow State Jewish Theatre) would direct a new film version of *The God of Vengeance* to be shot in simultaneous Yiddish, German, English and French versions. (Many early European sound films, like UFA's *The Blue Angel*, were made in separate foreign language editions for different markets.)

But soon, a wheel of fire would turn on *The God of Vengeance*. After the conflagration of World War II, the play became a prime example of pre-Holocaust art crushed in a post-Holocaust world.

The May 24, 1946 issue of the Jewish Telegraphic Agency's *Daily News Bulletin* (a press service for international Jewish news) includes pages of reports on post-War anti-Semitic outbreaks in Europe. There are gruesome news updates on riots and lethal incidents in Budapest, Rome, Prague, Graz and Munich, many of them involving attacks on Jews in displaced persons camps. But on page 4, there is also an announcement

from New York under the headline, "Sholem Asch
Bans His Own Play; Prohibits Staging *The God Of
Vengeance* In Any Language":

> New York, May 26. (JTA) – Sholem Asch, noted
> Jewish writer, today announced that he had
> prohibited the production of his play *The God Of
> Vengeance* in any language in the United States and
> in other countries. He explained the ban by stating
> that "the situation described in the play is dated
> and exists no longer."
>
> The play, which deals with the Jewish underworld
> in Poland, has been produced since 1907 in many
> languages throughout the world. It was given in
> English in Broadway theatres and was also
> performed in Yiddish. The disclosure that he had
> banned the play was made by Asch when
> information reached him that *The God Of Vengeance*
> was about to be produced in Spanish in Mexico
> City. He warned the Mexican theatre against
> producing the play and appealed to the cast to
> discontinue rehearsals.

Whatever its continuing reputation and popularity
in Asch's literary portfolio, *The God Of Vengeance*
was something of a distant, youthful work that lived
beyond its time. After World War I, Asch stopped
writing new plays and became an even more successful
novelist. By 1946, the theatre had not been his base for
decades (although he did collaborate on a few stage
adaptations of his novels). Asch could easily distance
himself from any potential controversies surrounding
this old play, especially since *The God Of Vengeance* was
the least of Asch's problems.

Of far greater concern to Asch and his post-War
international reputation was a trilogy of novels about
Christ. The first of these, *The Nazarene*, was published

in 1939, right at the start of World War II, and the second, *The Apostle*, appeared in English in 1943. When Asch banned *The God Of Vengeance*, he had already begun work on a third Christ novel, *Mary*, which came out in 1949.

Asch's theme in these novels was the common root of Judaism and Christianity, with the intent to foster religious reconciliation as Europe plunged through history's greatest anti-Semitic catastrophe. But Asch's Jewish readers were shocked at his admiring depiction of a Jewish Jesus. He was attacked as an apostate, for encouraging conversion and—not for the first time—defaming Judaism. The *Jewish Daily Forward* in New York, where Asch published his work ever since moving to America before World War I, fired him. He found a new outlet in another Yiddish paper, the *Morning Freedom*, but its communist affiliation eventually led to his being questioned by the House Un-American Activities Committee. In 1953, at the height of America's anti-communist storm, Asch left the United States to live in Israel. The estrangement between Asch and Jewish readers in both Yiddish and English was profound and never fully resolved in his lifetime. Beside the McCarthy-era threats to livelihood and safety sparked by his Christ novels, *The God Of Vengeance* was old news best left alone.

The Trial—

One of the loudest voices against Asch in the 1940's was Abraham Cahan, the long-time editor of New York's *Forward*. His attacks were particularly painful because from the 1907 U S premiere of *The God Of Vengeance* until *The Nazarene* appeared, Cahan had been one of Asch's greatest American advocates. He strongly supported the play during its 1923 obscenity

trial related to a successful English-language run on
Broadway starring Rudolph Schildkraut.

Although the trial's impact was comparatively
incidental to the full history of *The God of Vengeance*,
it has come back into theatrical consciousness due
to Paula Vogel's play *Indecent*. Apart from London
(where Yiddish-language performances by Lithuania's
Vilna Troupe in 1923 were initially approved,
but subsequently cancelled mid-run by the Lord
Chamberlain's Office, and an English-language staging
was dropped in 1946 after protests by the Deputy
Chief Rabbi), New York was the only other city where
a production of *The God of Vengeance* created serious
public outrage.

Already a major star in Berlin, Schildkraut first came
to America in 1910 to appear as a guest with the elite
German-language repertory company based at New
York's Irving Place Theatre, just off Union Square. He
moved permanently to New York in 1920, principally
to appear in silent films. (His actor son Joseph arrived
with him, and became an overnight Broadway success
in 1921, playing the title role in the Theatre Guild's
American premiere production of Molnar's *Liliom*.)

The first American translation of *The God of Vengeance*
had already been published in 1918 with a glowing
introduction by Cahan. Once Schidkraut settled
in New York, it seemed inevitable that *The God of
Vengeance* would receive a new English-language
production starring the actor for whom it was written.
Schildkraut was not fluent in English, but agreed
to learn the part phonetically and direct the play in
a staging based upon Rheinhardt's original. Harry
Weinberger, a prominent civil rights attorney (he
defended Emma Goldman in her deportation trial) and
pro bono counsel to the Provincetown Players, would
produce.

Performed in English, *The God of Vengeance* opened at
the 140-seat Provincetown Playhouse in Greenwich
Village on December 20, 1922. The reviews were
divided: generally negative for the script ("Somewhat
to our surprise, there are things which we cannot stand
to have said and done in the theatre," wrote Heywood
Broun in *The World*), but raves for Schildkraut. The
original run sold out, and moved to the larger, 425-seat
Greenwich Village Theatre in February 1923. Box Office
momentum continued, and only two weeks later,
Weinberger moved *The God of Vengeance* to Broadway's
1200-seat Apollo Theatre. Without prior warning,
during a performance on March 6 the producer, star
and full cast were arrested backstage. The previous
day, a grand jury had charged them with "unlawfully
advertising, giving, presenting, and participating in
an obscene, indecent, immoral, and impure drama or
play."

At trial, those supporting the play through written
testimonials included Eugene O'Neill, Elmer Rice and
Constantine Stanislavsky (who was on tour in America
with his Moscow Art Theatre, and knew *The God of
Vengeance* from its Russian productions). When the trial
concluded on May 28, a jury took 90 minutes to convict
all parties. Schildkraut and Weinberger were each
fined $200 (worth about $3000 in 2019), with everyone
else given suspended sentences. Weinberger continued
to pursue the case on appeal, and the NY State Court of
Appeals reversed all convictions in January 1925.

After the arrests on March 6, *The New York Times*
refused to carry any advertising for *The God of
Vengeance*. ("It seems hardly fair or becoming for *The
New York Times* to act as censor and pass judgment
on a play before the final decision of a jury has
been reached," Weinberger protested to the *Times'*
advertising manager.) But as before, controversy

was good for business. The play continued its
uninterrupted Broadway run, closing at the Apollo
on April 14, before moving yet again to a still larger
"Subway Circuit" venue, the 1500-seat Prospect
Theatre in The Bronx. In the final tally, there were
133 performances, at a time when *Variety* defined "hit
status" as anything that ran over 100 performances. (As
a point of comparison, a smash musical like the 1923
Ziegfeld Follies starring Fannie Brice ran twelve weeks
longer, for 233 performances.)

In that era's list of censored Broadway plays, *The God
of Vengeance* did considerably better than Shaw's *Mrs
Warren's Profession* (Shuttered on its opening night at
the Garrick Theatre in 1905), or Wedekind's *Spring
Awakening* (given a single performance in 1917 at the
39th Street Theatre, for which the Shuberts issued
a public apology). Only Mae West's *Sex* exceeded
The God of Vengeance's commercial success, running
an impressive 375 performances during the 1926-27
Broadway season before the Vice Squad shut it down.
Still, *The God of Vengeance* was a different case. Its
issues before the court in New York were not about
prurience, but social image, culture and religious
respect.

The fight against Asch was led by Joseph Silverman,
Rabbi Emeritus of Temple Emanuel, New York's
largest Reform Jewish Congregation and a bastion
of the city's prominent German-Jewish community.
(Silverman may have been a lone combatant. His legal
actions were opposed by other prominent rabbis,
including his successor at Temple Emanuel.) In part,
Silverman's campaign against *The God of Vengeance*
could be seen as a reflection of the long-simmering
social unease between New York's established,
assimilated and often wealthy "Western Jews" of
mostly German extraction, and the economically

poorer "Eastern Jews" of Russian-Polish heritage, who by the millions brought their rural "shetl" culture of more recent immigrant vintage to the New World.

Almost a perfect counterpart to the proper middle class home Yechel Tchaftchovitch built atop his brothel in *The God of Vengeance*, the play was regarded by "uptown" as the crude product of a rough "downtown" Yiddish community that the assimilated world could not accept. It was one thing for a Jewish drama showing prostitution, lesbianism and religious hypocrisy to run successfully in Yiddish theatres before Jewish audiences, but when it became a Broadway production in English, open to the Gentile world, Asch's play was "not for export".

From his 'downtown' pulpit as editor of the *Jewish Daily Forward*, Abraham Cahan led an attack on the trial. "Behind Rabbi Silverman are American Jews, who are up-to-date with their suits and dresses, but not in their understanding. They belong to that generation which believe that the highest duty of literature is to hide the truth. But times do not stand still, nor does the world."

Aside from reflecting class divisions within New York's Jewish community, Silverman's motivations were probably more complex. He had been a public voice in generating Jewish support for Armenians at the time of the Turkish massacres, and was concerned about rising xenophobia and anti-Semitism in the 1920's. This was the era of Henry Ford's publication of hate-filled anti-Semitic propaganda in the *Dearborn Independent*. Its mandatory distribution via Ford Auto dealerships across America yielded a weekly circulation of 900,000. Just a year after the *God of Vengeance* trial, Congress passed the Johnson-Reed Immigration act of 1924, which limited all immigrant entry to the United States through strict national origins quotas. However crude and elitist Silverman's actions appear regarding *The God of Vengeance*, he may have been motivated by seeking an indefinable balance between freedom of expression and a fear of pogroms to come.

The trial had no lasting impact, and well before the 1920's were over, *The God of Vengeance* was back on stage. When Maurice Schwartz revived the play in his Yiddish Art Theatre repertory both in New York and on tour, he followed up with stage adaptations of Asch novels, notably *Uncle Moses*, which concerns an overbearing and powerful sweatshop owner on the Lowest East Side who both supports and persecutes his immigrant employees. As with *The God of Vengeance*, Asch conjured a divided and unreconcilable Jewish community: What happens when the oppressor is one of our own? The roles of Uncle Moses and Yechel Tchaftschovitch are clearly related. Schwartz's remarkable performance in the film of *Uncle Moses* (The first Yiddish "talkie", shot in New York with its original Yiddish Art Theatre cast) gives some sense of what his Tschaftchovitz must have been like on stage.

The Legacy—

Interest in Yiddish drama has ebbed and flowed since World War II, probably reaching a peak when the 1978 Nobel Prize in Literature was awarded to Isaac Bashevis Singer, but *The God of Vengeance* was never lost. It has had four Off-Broadway productions since 1974. In 1999, it was staged in Atlanta by Joseph Chaikin, one of America's iconic experimental directors. A 2002 adaptation by David Margulies re-set it among Lower East Side immigrants and altered the context of Asch's play, but helped keep the title in circulation. The success of Vogel's *Indecent* on

Broadway and in regional theatres since 2017 pushed
The God of Vengeance's reputation still further, by
dramatizing the play's international history and giving
primacy to its lesbian scenes.

The translation given here was originally part of
a much larger project initiated by Richard Nelson.
Around 2003, Richard began to explore the Art Theatre
movement of the early twentieth century, using the
plays and critical writing of Harley Granville Barker
as a starting point. (Like Asch, Barker had his own
encounters with censorship. His play *Waste*, concerning
abortion rights, was written in 1906, the same year as
The God of Vengeance, but was not performed in public
until 1936.)

While exploring the multiple theatre revolutions of that
era—not only Barker, but Stanislavsky, Coupeau, the
"Little Theatre" movement in the United States, and
more—the serious side of Yiddish theatre emerged.
The repertory of Yiddish companies from Moscow to
Warsaw to London and on to New York was packed
with major classical and contemporary works of
Western drama. Produced alongside classics were
new plays by Goldfadden, Gordin, Ansky, Leivick,
Pinski, Hirschbein, Asch and more. The work on
stage went far beyond Yiddish theatre stereotypes of
broad musicals and uplifting nostalgia. Many of the
contemporary plays were not rural 'shtetl' comedies,
but stark urban dramas linked thematically to Russian
social themes.

Richard asked both Colin Chambers (The Royal
Shakespeare Company's former literary director)
and me to join him in creating new critical editions
of perhaps a half-dozen representative Yiddish
social dramas that could be produced and published
simultaneously. Despite considerable effort in both
London and New York, publishers and producers for

the total project were never found. All that came of it was Colin's new adaptation of Pinski's *Treasure*, which was staged in London in 2015 (subsequently published by Oberon Books in the UK), and this translation of Asch's *The God of Vengeance*.

To our great surprise, when we started work, the old defamation issues surrounding *The God of Vengeance* resurfaced. To create a new literal translation of Asch's original from which to start, we approached a distinguished member of a famous Yiddish literary family. The great Yiddish dramatists and their plays were part of her family's lore and passion. But when she read *The God of Vengeance*, her response was similar to Rabbi Silverman's and she immediately withdrew from the project. "Not for export." After that encounter, we went back to the first U S translation from 1918 by Isaac Goldberg, which was highly praised at the time for its fidelity to Asch.

Today, in an era of rising international anti-Semitism, it's impossible to ignore the non-theatrical issues that have defined *The God of Vengeance* for so many. The concerns brought out in the play's 1923 obscenity trial have undeniable counterparts with other modern Jewish authors. Apparently, there are three I B Singer novels (plus a memoir and short stories) that have been kept from English translation due to their frank sexual content and harsh portrayal of Jewish characters. One of those Singer novels still unpublished in English, *Yarme and Keyle*, concerns a Jewish sex slave trade involving gangsters and prostitutes. (It was serialized in the *Forward*, in Yiddish, between 1956 and 1957.) The novels of Holocaust survivor Edgar Hilsenrath, described in his 2019 *New York Times* obituary as "brutally satirical", were initially rejected by multiple publishers due to his unflattering characterization of Jews imprisoned within Nazi ghettos. In a defense of his portrayals, Hilsenrath wrote "In Germany, people want to make up to the Jews for what happened by idealizing them. The Jews in the ghetto were every bit as imperfect as human beings anywhere else."

Hilsenrath's self-defense echoed Asch's statement published before his 1923 obscenity trial in New York: "Jews do not need to clear themselves before anyone. They are as good and as bad as any race. I see no reason why a Jewish writer should not bring out the bad or good traits. I think that the apologetic writer, who tries to place Jews in a false, even though white light, does them more harm than good in the eyes of the Gentiles. I have written so many Jewish characters who are good and noble, that I cannot now, when writing of a "bad" one, make an exception and say that he is a Gentile." From the perspective of 1923, the Holocaust-to-come was almost inconceivable, but Asch was already on a path towards an unimaginably different post-War social context where his play's "situation...is dated and exists no longer."

In its overt melodrama and emotional excess, *The God of Vengeance is* dated. In its libertarian sexual attitude, it seems entirely fresh and contemporary. The reader (or actor) needs to breathe deeply in both worlds, pre and post Holocaust, to give this play a viable platform. Whatever its challenges, the grim poetic realism of *The God of Vengeance* stays convincingly alive, with truly vivid characters and an intensely complex interweaving of family and faith. The play remains a remarkable legacy of early twentieth century theatre.

New York, 2019

THE GOD OF VENGEANCE

CHARACTERS & SETTING

YEKEL TCHAFTCHOVITCH, *known casually as the "Uncle;" the owner of a brothel*

SARAH, *his wife; a former prostitute*

RIFKELE, *their daughter; an innocent girl of about 17*

HINDEL, *senior girl of the brothel, about 30, but looks much older*

MANKE, *second girl of the brothel; youngish*

REIZEL, *third girl of the brothel*

BASHA, *newly arrived at the brothel from the countryside*

SCHLOYME, *a pimp, engaged to* HINDEL, *26 and handsome.*

REB ALI, *a matchmaker and neighbor of the "Uncle"*

REB AARON VANKEV, *a religious scribe*

A STRANGER, *the father of* RIFKELE's *proposed husband*

A POOR WOMAN, *blind in one eye*

Poor men and women of the neighborhood

Time: Early in the 20th century.

Place: One of the larger towns in provincial Russia.

[This version is based upon Isaac Goldberg's 1918 translation.]

ACT ONE

(*The "Uncle's" private home on the ground floor of an old wooden house. Below the apartment, in the basement, is the brothel. A broken-down wooden staircase, whose noisy creaking announces all visitors, leads from the street to the apartment's main quarters—a large room with a low ceiling. The furniture is new, but somewhat cheap-looking, and doesn't fit with the old-fashioned building. The walls have been decorated with embroidered pictures on canvas that depict biblical scenes, such as "Adam and Eve at the Tree of Knowledge." These are the obvious handiwork of a teenage girl.*)

(*At the rear is the main doorway leading outside. At the right is the door of* RIFKELE's *bedroom. On each side of her door is a narrow bed piled high with sheets and bedding. Two low windows on the left are hung with curtains, and have old wooden shutters that can close from the inside. Below the windows are flowerpots and between them is a large cupboard. Along side a window is a bureau. [There is also a dining table with chairs, and a mirror. Another doorway leads to the rest of the apartment.]*)

(*The job of cleaning the room is almost done. Guests seem to be expected. Extra tables and benches have been set out that are piled high with bread, fruit and cake.*)

(*An afternoon in early spring*)

(SARAH *and* RIFKELE *are seen.* SARAH *is tall, slender and attractive. A certain coarseness and overbearing quality*

*is balanced by traces of her former beauty. She wears a
wig through which, at times, can be seen a lock of her own
alluring hair. She is dressed in a dignified, motherly manner,
but the effect is spoiled by a vulgar display of jewels. The
way she moves suggests that she is not quite liberated from
the manners of her past life as a prostitute.)*

*(*RIFKELE *is a captivating teenage girl, dressed very modestly
and neatly. She still wears short dresses, and her hair is tied
in long braids that hang over her shoulders. She is busy
decorating the room.)*

RIFKELE: *(Pinning paper flowers to the window curtains)*
There! Like that, Mama. And some on the mirror. Look
Mama. How's this?

SARAH: *(Arranging the table)* Finish up, Rifkele. Hurry
up. Your father's already gone to see if they'll bring
our Scroll.

RIFKELE: I can't wait. A house full of people. There'll be
music, singing. Won't there, Mama?

SARAH: There will. It's an important day—it's a great
gift. God sees that. Not just anyone pays for a new
Holy Scroll. Only important men. Respectable men.

RIFKELE: Any girls my age coming? Will there be
dancing? Mama, will there? *(Suddenly)* I don't have a
proper dress. Or the right shoes. *(Sticking out her shoes)*
You can't dance in shoes like these. Mama?

SARAH: Calm down. Wait until you're engaged. Next
Passover, I'll make you a beautiful long dress and buy
shoes you can dance in. Girls are coming, respectable
girls, young ladies. And you'll be nice to them.

RIFKELE: Why do I always have to wait until Passover?
I'm already grown up. *(Looking into the mirror)* Look
Mama. I'm a big girl. Look how long my braids are.
Manke says.... *(Interrupting herself)* Manke's coming,
too, isn't she, Mama?

SARAH: No, Rifkele. She isn't. Only nice, respectable girls. Good Jewish daughters, like you.

RIFKELE: But Mama, Manke sketched the Jewish Star I'm going to embroider on the Scroll's cover. A wreath of leaves and a garland of flowers. Wait til you see how beautiful it'll be. *(Points to the wall)* A hundred times prettier than those—

SARAH: *(Concerned)* My God, don't tell that to your father. He'll have a fit if he hears of that.

RIFKELE: Why Mama? It's for the Holy Scroll.

SARAH: You mustn't tell him.

(Footsteps)

SARAH: Sh-sh. Your father's coming.

YEKEL: *(Still outside; to someone in the street)* What? Do they think I'll bend over and kiss their asses? Not for anything! *(He enters the room. He is a tall, strong man of about 40. Stout. Dark complexion and a full head of hair, with a neatly trimmed black beard. He speaks loudly, with a rough voice, while making coarse gestures, like grabbing the lapels of the man to whom he is speaking. Despite this, face and overall manner have a certain frank geniality. To* SARAH*)* The bastards won't come! They don't have to! To hell with them. So I got some poor people to invite. Don't worry. You'll have 'guests' for all this cake, and the goose, Sarah. *(He sits down when he notices* RIFKELE.*)* Come here, Rifkele. Come to papa.

*(*SARAH *tries to hold back her anger and continues to set the table.)*

SARAH: Do they think they'll get shit on their boots coming here? My God, when they want to borrow a hundred rubles…or get something for their charities… they're not ashamed of you then. They think we're scum, but our money's clean enough.

YEKEL: She's excited already. Something new to worry about? Don't worry, this won't ruin anything that's yours. Rifkele, come to papa.

RIFKELE: *(Almost fearful and unwillingly, goes to him)* What, Papa?

YEKEL: Don't act like you're afraid of me, Rifkele. I'd never hurt you. *(He takes her hand)* Don't you like your father?

(RIFKELE nods "yes".)

YEKEL: Then why are you afraid of him?

RIFKELE: I don't know.

YEKEL: Don't be afraid of papa. He loves you. Very, very much. The Holy Scroll is coming today. It cost a lot of money, Rifkele. And it's for you. All for you.

(RIFKELE is silent. Pause)

YEKEL: When you're engaged, God willing, I'll buy your fiancé a gold watch with a chain…that weighs half a pound! Papa loves you so much!

(RIFKELE looks down, embarrassed. Pause)

YEKEL: Don't be so ashamed. There's nothing wrong about getting a man when the time is right. God wants it. It's nothing. Everyone gets engaged and married, Rifkele.

(RIFKELE is silent. Pause)

YEKEL: Come on, now. Don't you love papa?

RIFKELE: *(Nodding; softly)* Yes.

YEKEL: Then what should I buy you? Tell me, Rifkele.

(RIFKELE's silent.)

YEKEL: Tell me now. Don't be afraid. Your papa loves you. Come on, tell me like a good little girl. What should I buy you?

SARAH: *(Still setting the table)* Answer when your father speaks to you.

RIFKELE: I don't know…

SARAH: She wants a new long dress. And white shoes.

YEKEL: That's all? A dress and a pair of shoes?

(RIFKELE nods "yes".)

YEKEL: You deserve them! *(Taking a gold piece from his pocket, which jingles with coins)* Give this to Mama, and have her buy them for you.

(RIFKELE takes the coin and gives it to her mother.)

(Noise outside on the stairs; the poor guests have arrived.)

YEKEL: *(Turning to SARAH.)* See? *(He opens the door.)* And you said that no one would come! Our guests are here. Come in! Come in! *(Calling out towards the street)* Welcome!

(Some POOR people enter, men and women. The first enter a few at a time, and hesitantly, as if "stealing in", then more confidently in groups. They all greet YEKEL, some of them ironically, "putting him on".)

THE POOR: *(Variously)* Good morning, "Sir". "Mrs."

(SARAH puts on an apron and places in it loaves of bread and cakes she had stacked so carefully on the table. She distributes the food among her guests.)

A POOR MAN: Bless you. May you live to be a hundred.

A POOR WOMAN: May the Holy Scroll bring you good luck and bless your house!

YEKEL: *(Throwing slices of bread to the poor. To SARAH)* Give each of them a handful of cake…and a bottle of brandy, too. Something for home. They should know how I celebrate…. Why not? I can afford it.

A WOMAN: *(Blind in one eye. To the others)* This is what I call a home. Lucky them. Nobody leaves here hungry.

Soup if you're sick; a shirt if you need one. You think
it's like this with the rich across town?

*(*SARAH *pretends not to hear, but puts more food into the
woman's apron. The* BLIND WOMAN *holds out her apron
and continues.)*

THE BLIND WOMAN: They share here. It doesn't matter
who you are…what you do.

THE POOR: *(Among themselves)* True! It's true. May God
be so good to us.

YEKEL: *(Puting a handful of coins from his pocket into
Rifkele's apron)* Here, divide this among them.

*(*RIFKELE *distributes the money.)*

THE BLIND WOMAN: *(Getting excited)* And show me,
in the whole town, a girl as good as this! *(To the
other women in the crowd)* The rabbis don't have such
children. *(Softer, but loud enough for* YEKEL *and* SARAH
to hear) And brought up here? In a place like this such
a sweet girl. God only knows. *(Louder)* They guard her
like a treasure. Watch every step she takes. Just look at
her. *(Goes over to* YEKEL*)* Come on. Everyone knows. If I
had a rabbi for a son, I'd pick her for his bride.

OTHER POOR WOMEN: *(Among themselves)* The whole
town talks about her. Everybody knows.

YEKEL: Just wait 'til her wedding! Then, there'll be
a whole goose for each of you. With fresh herring.
And roubles! Lots of roubles, or my name isn't Yekel
Tchaftchovitch!

THE BLIND WOMAN: I'll even say this, it's like she'd
been raised inside a synagogue—Heaven forbid I use
that word here. Purer, more innocent than any child
from the best family.

OTHER POOR WOMEN: *(Variously)* Everybody knows.
Everybody talks about her.

YEKEL: *(Pouring glasses of brandy; blurts out before he realizes what he's saying)* Even though her father *is* Yekel Tschaftchovitch!

SARAH: *(Also handing out brandy glasses)* Look who you're trying to impress!

YEKEL: *(Pouring brandy; speaking passionately)* What difference does it make to me? Poor people or rich, everybody knows. The whole town knows! What *I* am, I am. *(Points to his wife.)* What *she* is, she is. It's true. All of it. But if a man spits one word against my daughter... Let anybody try.... I'll smash his head in with this bottle here. I don't care if it's the Rabbi himself. She's purer than his own daughter. *(Points to his throat:)* You can cut my throat if that's not true.

SARAH: *(Stops pouring brandy)* We've heard that before, Yekel. Enough. *(She picks up a broom in a corner.)* We have to clean up again for our guests. *(To the* POOR.*)* You understand, I'm sure.

POOR PEOPLE: *(Variously)* Yes. Yes, Mrs. May happiness and joy be yours forever. "Sir."

(The POOR *start to leave singly, offering exaggerated blessings.* YEKEL, *without* SARAH *noticing, throws them more food. The last woman calls to* RIFKELE; *loud enough for others to hear...)*

WOMAN: Rifkele, that scroll cover you've been sewing. Is it finished? Reb Ali and the Scribe will be here soon.

*(*RIFKELE *goes into her room.)*

SARAH: *(Sweeping the floor)* To have to brag in front of such people. Amazing. You think they're here to listen to you? You fill their bellies every day, they'll be here every day. People like that should be kept in their place. You treat everyone the same, slap them on the back. "Hello there, brother!" Well, we're not the same as them!

YEKEL: Ah, so now it's only the high and mighty we should bother to be seen with? Maybe you've forgotten who you are.

SARAH: Who I am? And who is that? Have we stolen anything? You're in business. Who doesn't have a business? You don't make anyone do what they don't want to do. You work hard, what's wrong with that? Just try to give them some of your hard earned cash and see if they take it.

YEKEL: They'll take it, all right, but they'll still look at you like you're a dog. At the synagogue you'll have the last seat. They'd never call you up to alter to read from the Holy Book.

SARAH: Do you really believe they're better than you? You don't need their handouts. Here's how the world works today: If you've got the money, even a Jew as pious as Reb Ali comes to you, to your home—with his hand open. As good a Jew as Reb Ali. And no questions asked. No one asks if you got it by stealing or killing, so long as you have the cash. That's all that matters.

YEKEL: Get off your high horse, Sarah, before you fall and break your neck. Know your place. Please. You have a home. Stay in it. You have bread. Eat. But don't go where you're not wanted. Every smart dog soon learns to accept the length of his leash. (Leaving the table) This whole thing's begun to worry me. I don't think we'll get what we're hoping for.

SARAH: You call yourself a man? Shame on you! I'm just a woman, but I can tell myself, "the past is the past." Goodbye. Over. And whoever you're ashamed of, he's gone, too. That's how the world works. If it didn't, everyone'd be walking around with bowed heads. (Coming closer to YEKEL) Soon you'll just be someone with money. You'll close up shop and no one says a word. No one needs to know what we were.

YEKEL: *(Thoughtful)* That would be for the best…. *(Pause.)* Buy some horses, smuggle them across the border, like Eisikl Fuhrman did. And become respectable; stop having people eyeing me like a thief.

SARAH: *(Considering the idea)* Just the same, it'd be a shame to just close down here. You'd never make such good money from your horses. Here, at least, it's all cash.

YEKEL: True.

(SARAH goes into the next room and returns with a tray of plates. She begins arranging them on the table.)

SARAH: Look at the daughter we have. Thank God, what a good girl, better than all the daughters of the best families in town. She'll marry a proper man; raise a respectable family. That's true, isn't it? So then, what's so wrong?

YEKEL: *(Standing up)* Sure, with you as her example? Go ahead. Let Manke sneak up from downstairs to see her! Let her move in up here!

SARAH: Stop it! I asked Manke once to come up and teach Rifkele to embroider on canvas. Rifkele's growing up; you can't ignore that. Has she any friends? You won't let her set foot in the street. *(Pause.)* But if you really don't want her with Manke, she won't.

YEKEL: No, I don't want her with Manke! You hear me? I don't! I don't want her around those girls. *(Points to the cellar)* My home is kept separate from the business, like what's clean is kept from dirt! Downstairs is a brothel, and here lives a pure girl, worthy of marrying the best of men. Do you hear? *(Bangs the table)* A pure, virtuous virgin lives here! Keep the two places apart!

(Footsteps are heard outside.)

SARAH: All right. I will. Just calm down. *(Listening)* Sh-sh. People are coming. It's Reb Ali.

*(*SARAH *pushes some hair under her wig, and pulls off her apron while* YEKEL *strokes his beard and straightens his coat. They stand by the door, expectantly. The door opens wide as* SHLOYME *and* HINDEL *enter.* SHLOYME *is tall, well-built, wears long boots and a short coat. He has a cunning manner about him, reinforced by sinister eyes that blink as he speaks.* HINDEL *looks old for her age, with a pale face. She wears clothes in a style too young for her age. They are both entirely comfortable and at home here.)*

YEKEL: *(To* SARAH*)* These aren't guests! *(To* SHLOYME*)* I don't do business here. Down there. I'll come down soon.

SHLOYME: What's the hurry to get rid of us? Already he's ashamed of us?

YEKEL: Why are you here?

SHLOYME: It's a big day for you, isn't it? So we wanted to wish you luck. Old friend to old friend.

SARAH: Look at who calls you friend!

YEKEL: Once upon a time we were. From today that's over. You want to talk business? Fine, but all that's downstairs. *(Pointing below.)* Here, I don't know you and you don't know me. You're welcome to a shot of brandy.

*(*YEKEL *pours* SHLOYME *a drink.)*

YEKEL: Drink up. Someone might come in.

SHLOYME: *(Taking the drink, to* HINDEL*:)* See what I was saying about marriage? You become someone, become as good as other people, can even get Holy Scrolls written. Not like us folks, not like us trash. *(To* YEKEL*)* And I'm going to follow in your footsteps, Yekel. I'm going to get married myself—to this thing here. *(He* *points to* HINDEL.*)* She'll make a hell of a housewife, won't she? You can see that. Stick a wig on her and she'll be the picture of a Rabbi's wife. As I live and die….

YEKEL: Congratulations. What do you know. So you're getting married. And when's the wedding?

SARAH: Who cares about them. You'll talk to anyone. They're nobody. Reb Ali and the Scribe will be here any minute.

SHLOYME: When's the wedding? What wedding? Our kind don't have weddings. We'll get a couple of girls and open our own house—that'll be our wedding. What are we—rabbis? The girls are going to be special, classy. Hot-blooded. *(Winks at* YEKEL*)* Otherwise it doesn't pay, does it?

YEKEL: What do you want from me?

SHLOYME: From you? Not much. *(Points to* HINDEL*)* She works for you, right? But she's my girl. And you owe her money.

*(*SHLOYME *takes a notebook from* HINDEL.*)*

SHLOYME: From now on, you pay me. Today—a little. Ten rubles. Take it off what you owe. *(Slaps the book closed)* She needs the money. She wants to buy herself a hat.

YEKEL: Downstairs! Down there. I'll be down soon, and we'll take care of business down there. I don't even know you here. Here I'll do no business with you!

SHLOYME: What do I care? Above. Below. I know everyone downstairs. And upstairs, too. Same thing. Same thing.

YEKEL: Get out! Get out! Do you hear me? People are coming.

SARAH: Go to hell! They want to spoil everything. *(Looks scornfully at* HINDEL*)* But I shouldn't let her upset me. She's just a whore.

HINDEL: Just a whore? Why don't you go down there yourself, then?

SHLOYME: Or send her daughter. What a great business you'd do then.

YEKEL: *(Moving towards* SHLOYME*)* Attack me—go ahead. *(Pointing)* Attack her, too. We're your kind. But don't dare even breathe my daughter's name. Understand? *(Coming closer to* SHLOYME*)* I'll rip your guts out. Hear me? She doesn't know you, and you don't know her.

SHLOYME: But I can get to know her. The daughter of a fellow businessman. Paths cross.

YEKEL: *(Grabbing* SHLOYME *by the throat)* I'll rip your guts out! You can hit me in the face, kick me, go ahead, but don't speak my daughter's name.

*(*SHLOYME *and* YEKEL *start to fight.)*

SARAH: *(Running to them)* God help me! They're scum. They're not worth fighting! Someone could walk in! Yekel! Reb Ali and the Scribe—Yekel, For God's sake!

*(*SARAH *drags* YEKEL *off* SHLOYME.*)*

SARAH: What are you doing?

(Footsteps on the staircase outside.)

YEKEL: Let go of me. I've had enough of—

REB ALI: *(Off:)* We're here Scribe. This is the home of the Scroll's donor. *(He opens the door, peers in, thrusting his large head into the room. He has a pipe.)* What's all the noise about? In the home of a man who has a Holy Scroll—there must be joy, happiness. No arguing. *(To* THE SCRIBE:*)* This way, please, Scribe.

(When YEKEL *hears* REB ALI's *voice, he releases* SHLOYME. SARAH *helps* SHLOYME *up and gives him paper money from her stocking. She pushes him and* HINDEL *towards the door, where they encounter* REB ALI *and* THE SCRIBE *in the doorway. The two religious men back away from* HINDEL, *leaving as much room as possible for her and* SHLOYME.*)*

SHLOYME: *(To* HINDEL *as they leave)* Take a peek at the folks he's got visiting him now. Next, it'll be Yekel for mayor.

(They are gone.)

*(*REB ALI *is a short, heavy man who speaks quickly and ingratiatingly. He seems to have a high opinion of himself and is very much at home in this house.)*

REB ALI: My apologies, Scribe. My apologies. *(Whispers to* SARAH *and* YEKEL*)* Is this any way to behave? Enough! People are coming and—

*(*THE SCRIBE *enters. He is a tall, old man whose thin body is enveloped in a wide overcoat. His beard is long, white and sparse. He wears glasses, and has an air of cold aloofness and mystery.)*

REB ALI: *(Pointing to* YEKEL*)* This is the donor of the Scroll.

*(*THE SCRIBE *extends his hand to* YEKEL, *while looking him over.)*

THE SCRIBE: May God grant you peace, fellow Jew.

*(*YEKEL, *uncertain, suddenly thrusts his hand towards* THE SCRIBE. SARAH *steps reverently aside.)*

REB ALI: *(At the table, pulling back a chair.)* Be seated, Scribe. *(To* YEKEL:*)* Sit down.

*(*THE SCRIBE *sits.* YEKEL, *increasingly uncertain, sits opposite him, next to* REB ALI.*)*

REB ALI: *(To* THE SCRIBE:*)* This is the gentleman for whom I ordered the Holy Scroll. *(He helps himself to*

a brandy, pouring first for THE SCRIBE.*)* He has no son,
so he wishes to honor the Lord our God with a Holy
Scroll of the Law. Such is the custom among the people
of Israel, and a very beautiful one, too. We must help
him. To your health, Scribe. *(He extends his hand to* THE
SCRIBE, *then to* YEKEL.*)* To your health, host. Today, you
are the host of our celebration.

(YEKEL, *even more uncertain, extends his hand to* REB ALI.
REB ALI *drinks.* SARAH *moves towards the table and pushes
jelly preserves towards* REB ALI, *but* YEKEL *pulls her sleeve
and signals that she should back away.)*

REB ALI: *(After drinking; turns to* THE SCRIBE*)* Drink,
Scribe. *(To* YEKEL:*)* Drink host. Today, rejoice. God has
favored you with the means of having a Holy Scroll
written. It is a divine honor. A very great one.

THE SCRIBE: *(Holding his glass; to* REB ALI, *referring to*
YEKEL*)* Who is this man?

REB ALI: What does it matter? He's a Jew. So what if
he's no scholar, but must all men be scholars? A Jew
wants to earn God's blessing. We must befriend him.
(To YEKEL.*)* Drink. To your happiness.

THE SCRIBE: Does he know how to care for the Holy
Scroll?

REB ALI: And why not? He's a Jew, isn't he? And what
Jew doesn't know the importance of a Scroll? *(He
drinks.)* Your health! Your health! May the Lord bless
his people.

THE SCRIBE: *(Extending his hand to* YEKEL*)* Your health,
host. *(Admonishing him.)* And know that the Holy
Scroll, it is a wondrous possession. The whole world
rests upon its word of Law. Every scroll—a copy of the
tablets received by Moses on Mount Saini. Each line
is penned in purity and faith. Where the Scroll rests,

God himself rests. So we must guard it against every impurity. Man, you must know that a Holy Scroll....

YEKEL: (*Awed; stammering*) Sir, sir— I want you to know the truth, sir—the real truth. I am a poor sinner. Sir, you must know that—

REB ALI: (*Cutting* YEKEL *off; to* THE SCRIBE) The man is sincerely repentent. It's our duty to befriend him. Jewish law tells us so. Of course he understands the importance of a Holy Scroll. He's a Jew, after all. (*To* YEKEL:) One must revere a Holy Scroll. Greatly revere—as if a great Rabbi moved into your house. Under your roof, there will be no profanity. It must live amid purity. (*Speaks to* SARAH, *but not directly at her.*) Where the Torah rests, no woman may remove her wig.

(SARAH *pushes her hair more securely under her wig.*)

REB ALI: Nor may she touch the scroll with her bare hands. In return, no evil shall come to a home that shelters a Scroll. Such a home will prosper and be blessed. (*To* THE SCRIBE:) What are you concerned about? That he doesn't know this? They're Jews.

(SARAH *nods.*)

THE SCRIBE: (*To* YEKEL:) You hear, sir, that the whole world rests upon the Scroll. The fate of our race lies rolled up in that parchment. With one word, with a single word, God forbid, you can desecrate Holy Law, and bring down upon all Jews a terrible misfortune. God forbid!

(YEKEL *stands.*)

YEKEL: Sir, I must confess everything. (*Comes nearer to* REB ALI.) I know that you are a holy man. I am not worthy, Reb Ali, of your being here, under my roof. I am a sinner. (*Pointing to* SARAH:) *She* is a sinner. We have no right to a Holy Scroll. But inside that room *(Points to the door)* —for her sake—

(YEKEL goes to RIFKELE's room and gently brings her forward by the hand. She is holding the velvet Scroll cover she is embroidering with a Jewish Star in gold thread.)

YEKEL: Sir, she— *(Pointing to RIFKELE)* —she may have the Holy Scroll. She is as pure as the Scroll itself. I ordered it for her. Look at the cover my daughter's embroidering. She may, because her hands are pure. I, sir, *(Striking his chest)* I promise not touch your Holy Law. *(Points to SARAH)* She will not touch your Scroll. She— *(Rests his hand on RIFKELE's head)* will carry it. It will be placed in her room. *(To RIFKELE:)* And when you are married and leave my house, take the Scroll with you to your husband's home.

REB ALI: *(To YEKEL:)* Let's be clear, when you marry her off, you'll give her the Holy Scroll as her dowry? Isn't that it?

YEKEL: Reb Ali, when my daughter is married, her dowry will be a pile of money. And I'll say to her, "Get out of your father's house and forget—forget your father—forget your mother—and have pure children, Jewish children, just like every Jewish daughter." That's what I'll say to her.

REB ALI: But the Holy Scroll will be a wedding present to your son-in-law. That's right, isn't it? The world, you see, Reb Aaron, still has pious Jews. Here is a man with a daughter, and he has a Scroll written for her future husband. How beautiful is that? How—good. I tell you, Reb Aaron, the spirit of Israel, the Jewish— ahem—ah— *(Smacks his lips.)*

(YEKEL brings RIFKELE back to her room and closes the door.)

YEKEL: Sir, the simple, plain truth. We're alone. My
wife may hear this. We are sinners. I know that God
will punish us. Let him punish. I accept that. Let Him
cripple me, disfigure me. Let him take all my money
so I will have to beg from door to door. Please God—
not that. *(Quieter:)* Sir, when a man has a son who
goes bad—. To hell with him. But a daughter, sir. If a
daughter falls, it's as if the mother had sinned in her
grave. So I went to the synagogue, and approached
this man *(Points to Reb Ali)* and said to him, "Give me
something that'll protect my home from evil." So he
said to me, "Have a Holy Scroll written and place it
in your home." Sir, as for us, our souls are damned
already. It's for her. And in her room I'll place the
Scroll, for her to have as a friend. As for us, we dare
not—we must—

*(REB ALI and THE SCRIBE whisper to themselves and
gesture towards YEKEL. He and SARAH stand and wait
expectantly at the table. Pause)*

THE SCRIBE: *(After brielfly considering the situation)* And
where are the guests in honor of the Holy Scroll?

REB ALI: We'll go back to the synagogue and gather
a quorum of Jews. It won't be hard to find enough
willing guests. *(He stands to pour more brandy and slaps
YEKEL on the back.)* God will help you! Rejoice, Host!
The Lord God protects all who truly repent. Don't
worry. You'll marry your girl to some scholar. Find
yourself a poor student for a son-in-law and support
him while he sits and studies religion all day. And so
win God's forgiveness. *(Pause)* I've really been thinking
about it, and have a boy in mind—a good catch; a real
head on his shoulders. His father's highly regarded.
(Suddenly) It's a big dowry?

YEKEL: Sir, take all I own. I'll let you strip me bare.
Take everything; everything. And I'll say to my girl,

"Forget your mother, forget your father!" And I'll send her and her husband whatever they need; they don't even have to know where it all comes from. "Here's your food and drink. Keep studying your holy books. I don't know you. You don't know me."

REB ALI: It'll all work out. The Scroll wll see to that. Come, Scribe. Come, host, let's go to the synagogue. We'll hunt out a quorum and celebrate the Holy Scroll. *(To* THE SCRIBE:*)* Do you see, Reb Aaron? A Jew, even if he sins, is still a Jew. A Jewish soul—seeks a pious scholar for a son-in-law. *(To* YEKEL:*)* Don't you worry. God will help you. He loves a repentant sinner. But you must give generously to the religious schools. If one can't study the Holy Law himself, then at least support those who can, for the whole world rests upon the Holy Law. *(To* THE SCRIBE:*)* Is that not so, Reb Aaron? And why not? *(Pointing to* YEKEL*)* I knew his father. A fine man. A wagon driver. Handsome, too. Believe me, God will help this fellow, and he'll become as good a Jew as anyone. *(To* YEKEL:*)* The most important thing is to repent deep in your heart—that is—abandon the sinful path you've followed 'til now, and give generously to the students of our Holy Word.

YEKEL: *(Summoning courage, to* REB ALI:*)* Just let me make a little more money, Reb Ali, so I can give my daughter a real dowry. And my name isn't Yekel Tchaftchovitch if I don't close my business soon. I'll sell horses, like my father, may he rest in peace. I'll get together a stable and take them to the Lovitch Fair. And my new son-in-law will be sitting inside there, studying sacred law. I'll come home for the Sabbath, sit down right here, and listen to him read from the Commentaries. If I'm lying, my name isn't Yekel.

REB ALI: Don't worry, it's all right. The Lord God will help you. Yes, I know he will. Isn't that true, Reb Aaron?

THE SCRIBE: Who knows? Ours is a God of mercy and forgiveness, but He is also a God of retribution and vengeance. Well, it's getting late. Let's go to the synagogue. *(He leaves.)*

YEKEL: What was he whispering to you?

REB ALI: It's all right. Don't worry. God will help you. He *must* help you. Come, come and take your Holy Scroll home and rejoice.

(About to leave, YEKEL *hesitates.)*

REB ALI: What? Do you need to talk to your wife? Tell her to prepare for our return with the Scroll?

SARAH: *(To* REB ALI*)* Everything is ready, Reb Ali. Everything.

REB ALI: Then what are you waiting for? The Scribe has already gone.

YEKEL: *(At the door; uncertain; points to himself)* Will you really be seen with me? In the street?

REB ALI: Come, if the Lord forgives you, surely we can, too.

YEKEL: *(Enthusiastically)* You're a good man, Reb Ali. *(He is about to embrace him, but stops himself.)* A good man—may I become one, too.

*(*REB ALI *and* YEKEL *leave together. Evening. Shadows)*

SARAH: *(Beginning to clean again and re-arrange the table.)* Rifkele, come help a little. They'll soon be coming with the Scroll.

RIFKELE: *(In her bedroom doorway; uncertain)* Has father left already?

SARAH: Yes. He went back to the synagogue with Reb Ali and the Scribe. The Rabbi will soon be coming, and the other guests, too.

RIFKELE: *(Showing her the scroll cover)* See how nice I've embroidered it.

SARAH: Yes, yes, I see. But comb your hair. Get dressed. The guests will be here soon. The Rabbi and—

RIFKELE: I'll get Manke to come upstairs and comb me. I love it when she combs me. She does it so beautifully. Makes my hair so smooth. And her hands are so cool. *(She takes something and taps the floor, calling:)* Manke! Manke!

SARAH: *(Frightened)* Rifkele! What are you doing? Don't! Your father will have a fit! It doesn't look good, spending you time with Manke. You're seen as a young woman now, someone's possible—wife. Virtuous. We've just been talking about possible husbands. Good matches—students, scholars.

RIFKELE: But I love Manke so much!

SARAH: I said, it's wrong to spend your time with Manke. You're a good girl; you must be seen with good, respectable girls. We're making a match for you, an excellent match. Reb Ali is going to introduce your father to him. *(She goes to the next room.)* We should wash, dress, put on our best clothes. The guests could be here any minute.

RIFKELE: A husband? What kind of husband, Mama?

SARAH: *(From the other room)* A sweet young man. A wonderful student, from a good family.

(MANKE enters quietly through the outside door. She wags a finger playfully at RIFKELE. RIFKELE goes toward her, cautiously walking backwards, signaling her to come into the room. The room is growing dark. RIFKELE falls into MANKE's arms.)

RIFKELE: *(To SARAH in the other room.)* Is he handsome, mama?

(MANKE *kisses* RIFKELE *passionately.*)

SARAH: *(From the other room)* Yes, Rifkele! Handsome, with long, jet-black hair and a satin coat. And a velvet cap, like a Rabbi. He's the son of a Rabbi, Reb Ali said.

(RIFKELE, *embraced by* MANKE, *and caressing her cheeks:*)

RIFKELE: And where will we live, Mama?

SARAH: *(From the other room)* In your room—with the Holy Scroll. He'll live with you and study Holy Law.

(RIFKELE, *in* MANKE'*s arms:*)

RIFKELE: And will he love me, Mama?

SARAH: *(From the other room)* He will. He will love you so much. And you'll have children yourself. Beautiful children, pure and innocent—

END OF ACT ONE

ACT TWO

(The cellar-brothel. Rain coming through the window)

(In the background a number of curtained-off "compartments" with beds. Sofas, table, benches, etc. Overhead lamps. SHLOYME *sleeps on a sofa.)*

(Night. Spring)

*(*HINDEL *enters quietly, trying not to wake* SHLOYME.*)*

SHLOYME: *(Waking up and looking around:)* You? Why aren't you out?

HINDEL: It started raining.

*(*SHLOYME *sits up.)*

SHLOYME: So you're talking to me. So I'm forgiven?

HINDEL: I wasn't angry.

SHLOYME: I don't care whether you're angry or not. *(He lies back down.)*

*(*HINDEL *looks around. Goes to a curtained-off area, listens, then turns back to* SHLOYME.*)*

HINDEL: Shloyme, I'm not going back out. Talk to me, no one's here. Tell me, as there's a God in Heaven, tell me—are you going to marry me?

SHLOYME: Your "majesty" —go hide your money inside your shirt, run to "Uncle" Yekel and complain that I take everything you make—that you can't even buy yourself a hat—.

HINDEL: Yes, I did that. What did you expect me to do? I give you the clothes off my back and you start flirting with that yellow bitch. I'll throw acid in her face. Smell her breath—it makes you sick. What could you be thinking? Is she want you want?

SHLOYME: Get away from me! You want this [fist] in your face?

HINDEL: Go ahead! Rip the skin off my body while you're at it. *(Holds out her arm)* You've already covered me black and blue. *(Shows other arm)* Go ahead, hit, pinch, whatever you want. Just tell me, now, on the memory of your father and truly as you pray for his soul, will you marry me?

SHLOYME: *(Stretching:)* I did want to. Now I don't.

HINDEL: So it's no. Fair enough. Now I know. What do I owe you? How much? A coat? Is that enough? Don't try to cheat me. *(She walks away.)*

SHLOYME: Fine! Get someone else. Knowing you, it won't take long either.

HINDEL: I'm glad you're so concerned about me.

SHLOYME: 'Oh I am.' Do what you want. *(Pause)* How about getting me a glass of tea?

(HINDEL gets SHLOYME a glass of tea and goes and sits in her "compartment".)

HINDEL: Do you like her? You do, don't you. Well you'll have your hands full with her. She's going to need those skinny breasts padded. You'll need to pay a dentist to put a whole new set of teeth in that mouth, there's the stilts to make her human-size. You'll need a barrel-organ to take along with her. I always thought your future was as an organ grinder. I'll throw you a couple of kopeks myself, from the window—

SHLOYME: Shut up.

HINDEL: And if I don't?

SHLOYME: You want a smack. in the face?

HINDEL: Try it. Those days are over. You hit me now, and you'll get back worse.

SHLOYME: And who's going to do that? Who's going to hit me back?!

(SHLOYME grabs HINDEL's purse she has been fiddling with and opens it.)

SHLOYME: What's this? *(He takes out a photo.)* Moyshe the locksmith? So, this is your protector? Since when?

HINDEL: None of your business.

SHLOYME: It is my business!

(SHLOYME slaps HINDEL, she cries.)

SHLOYME: Moyshe the locksmith? Trading photographs behind my back. *(Silence)* And I knew nothing of this? Hindel? Hindel? Come here.

(No reply)

SHLOYME: Hindel! Come here, I tell you! Do you hear me!

(HINDEL gets up and goes to SHLOYME, hiding her face in her handkerchief.)

SHLOYME: Have you spoken to Manke?

HINDEL: *(Crying:)* Yes.

SHLOYME: And what does she say?

HINDEL: *(Crying:)* If we start our own place, she'll come.

SHLOYME: And you believe her?

HINDEL: *(Drying her eyes)* Yes. But she doesn't want to come alone. She has a friend.

SHLOYME: Good. You can't even pay the rent with one girl.

HINDEL: What we need is a fresh young one.

SHLOYME: Sure. That would be nice. And how are we going to get one?

HINDEL: I've got my eye on a girl—as beautiful as the day is long, and still untouched.

SHLOYME: *(Curious:)* You think you can get her?

HINDEL: I think so.

SHLOYME: A girl from another house?

HINDEL: No. A virgin.

SHLOYME: How do you know her?

HINDEL: She comes here every night to see Manke. Sneaks out. Unseen. Something pulls her here. She can't get enough.

(RIFKELE calls from the window:)

RIFKELE: Pssst! Is my father down there?

HINDEL: No.

(RIFKELE disappears.)

SHLOYME: Her? Yekel's daughter? She's be a gold mine.

HINDEL: Sh-sh. She's coming.

(RIFKELE runs in, excited.)

RIFKELE: Where's Manke? In there? *(Points to a curtained-off compartment)* There with a…?

(HINDEL nods.)

(RIFKELE approaches MANKE's "room" and listens, excited:)

SHLOYME: *(To HINDEL, quietly:)* Tomorrow I'll look at that house on Pivna Street.

HINDEL: And when will we get married?

SHLOYME: First the house.

HINDEL: How much will the Rabbi charge to marry us?

SHLOYME: As long as there's enough left to buy some furniture. The place can't look like shit.

(YEKEL *bursts in. Dressed in orthodox clothes, shaking the rain from his hat)*

YEKEL: My luck. It has to rain. *(Suddenly sees* RIFKELE *and explodes with rage:)* You? You here?!

(YEKEL *grabs and shakes* RIFKELE:)

YEKEL: What are you doing down here?

RIFKELE: *(Frightened:)* Mama…Mama told me to…to… *(Cries)* Don't hit me!

YEKEL: Your mother sent you?! Your mother!!!

(YEKEL *starts to drag* RIFKELE *out.)*

YEKEL: She'll ruin you. That woman can't help herself. She wants her daughter to be what she was!

RIFKELE: *(Crying:)* Don't hit me, Papa!

YEKEL: I'll teach you to listen to your father!

(YEKEL *drags* RIFKELE *out, crying is heard off.)*

SHLOYME: Yekel—the virtuous. Who thinks he's too good to have a daughter who's a whore.

(Upstairs—banging and weeping of a woman.)

SHLOYME: He's giving it to his wife now. That's the way. Biff. Bang.

HINDEL: He's right. A mother needs to watch her daughter. Whatever you were, you were, but once you're married and have a baby, watch over it. You'll see. If God gives us a baby, I'll know what to do. My daughter will be as pure as a saint, with cheeks as red as beets. No one will lay a hand on her. And she'll marry someone respectable, and have a proper wedding.

SHLOYME: *(Slapping her across the shoulder:)* We'll see about that, all in due time. But talk to Rifkele now. Work on her. Otherwise—we have nothing.

HINDEL: I know what to do. I know what to say.

SHLOYME: Then—we'll see. *(Silence)* If she bites, pull her in and bring her right to me, she—.

(YEKEL enters, angry.)

YEKEL: We're closing up. It's raining. Even a dog won't stick his snout down here tonight. *(Looks to SHLOYME:)* You two—enough whispering. We're closed. *(Calls outside)* Reizel! To bed! Basha! Get to bed!

(From off: shouts of "In a minute" and "We're coming!")

(HINDEL points to YEKEL and signals for SHLOYME to leave. SHLOYME starts to go, stops near YEKEL and they look each other in the face.)

YEKEL: Move. I've closed. You've schemed enough.

SHLOYME: When did you become so respectable?

YEKEL: Get out. Move. I'll talk to you later.

SHLOYME: Go to hell.

(HINDEL runs to SHLOYME.)

HINDEL: Shloyme, go home. Please. Do you hear me? Go home!

(SHLOYME leaves after another look at YEKEL.)

SHLOYME: What an asshole. *(He is gone.)*

YEKEL: He's the last thing I need now. *(Points to HINDEL)* And you! Why don't you take your tired old carcass and start that place of your own.

HINDEL: You need more than tired carcasses to start a place. You need young girls—.

YEKEL: *(Calls:)* Reizel! Basha!

(They enter from the street, wet. YEKEL *goes.)*

BASHA: I love the smell of rain. Makes me think of home—and that smell of drying apples. This is the first May rain.

HINDEL: What are you crazy? Standing out in that rain. Who do you think is going to come by? No one's out there, it's pouring. *(She goes to her compartment and begins to pack up.)*

REIZEL: I don't care who comes by. I've earned enough for the month. We stood under the eaves, smelling the rain, washing the winter out of our hair. *(To* HINDEL*:)* Here, smell—doesn't it smell sweet.

BASHA: In my village, the first sorrel will be sprouting. And with the first May rain, they make sorrel soup. The goats will be out in the meadow. The rafts on the stream. And Franek rounding up the Gentile girls to go dancing at the inn. The women will be baking cheesecake for the holidays. *(Silence)* You know what? I'm going to buy myself a new summer coat and go home for the holidays. *(Goes to her compartment and comes back with a hat)* And this. If I walked off the train in this—they'd be so jealous. Wouldn't they? If only my father were dead.

REIZEL: Why? What would he do to you?

BASHA: Kill me on the spot. He's come at me with a crowbar. Once he caught me dancing with Franek at the tavern, he hit me with it. I still have the scar. *(She shows her.)* I come from a good family. My father's a butcher. I had suitors. *(In a whisper:)* They tried to match me up with Nottke, a meat cutter. I've still got the ring. *(Shows her)* He gave it to me at the Feast of Tabernacles. Maybe he didn't want to either, but I couldn't marry him.

REIZEL: Why not?

BASHA: I just couldn't. He smelled of meat. His name is Pshorik. Think of marrying a Pshorik and having new little Pshoriks every year. Yuck.

REIZEL: And this is better?

BASHA: Here at least I'm free. I've got nice clothes and dress well. Better clothes even than the rich girls in my village. *(She goes and gets a brown dress.)* When I walk down Marshalkovski Street in this—the looks I get. I know what they're thinking. I know what they want. If only I could come home wearing this, step off the train… *(Pretends to stroll)* God they'd die of jealousy. They'd keel over on the spot.

REIZEL: *(Adjusts BASHA's dress and hat:)* Like this. Raise your head higher. They'd…never have to know you came from a place like this. Let them think you're from one of the big fancy houses where you meet a count who has fallen in love with you…

HINDEL: *(From her room, still packing:)* And what's wrong with a place like this? Those girls in those big houses are no better than us… We do the same job. We're no different than anyone else—even girls from the best families aren't really any better. This is what we do to eat. And trust me, when one of us gets married—we're more faithful to our man than any of them. Maybe because we've seen what men are like, we know what to expect.

BASHA: *(Still looking at herself:)* I wonder if they'd even recognize me. Maybe not right away, but then… You know my mother died when she heard. It was too much for her. I've never even visited her grave. *(Suddenly stops)* Sometimes I see her. Sometimes in my dreams. In a shroud, covered in thorns—my sins. And she grabs me by the hair.

REIZEL: Your mother? You really see her? What does she look like? Is she white like a ghost?

HINDEL: Shut up, both of you. Telling stories about the dead at this time of night. Anyway—no dead people will come here. Our boss has a Holy Scroll upstairs. *(Pause)* What's wrong with what we do? *(She joins the girls.)* Wasn't our boss's wife like us—for years? But she got married. And she's respectable. She observes the laws that good Jewish daughters must keep. Her girl's pure. Our boss—respected. He's generous. Gives more than anyone to the poor. He's even had a Holy Scroll written.

REIZEL: But you're not supposed to read from a Scroll like that. And daughters of such mothers become what the mothers were. They'll get pulled down as if by a magnet, an Evil Force, that drags them into mud.

HINDEL: Who told you that?

REIZEL: An old fortune teller—a sorceress told me. Such a daughter is under a spell, she's cursed.

HINDEL: That's a lie! Who's that old gypsy who told you that? I'll scratch her eyes out. There is a God in Heaven. We have a God in Heaven.

(MANKE enters from her compartment, half-dressed.)

MANKE: What? Where are the customers?

REIZEL: Manke, you're just in time. *(Points to HINDEL:)* She almost got me believing in God. Where's your "guest"?

MANKE: He fell asleep.

REIZEL: Some generous land owner, I hope. So he can buy us drinks.

MANKE: I wish. He's a fool. Third time he's here. He keeps wanting to know—who's my father, who's my mother? What does he think—he's marrying me? He loves to snuggle his face into these [her breasts]. Like a baby in his mother's arms. Has Rifkele been here?

HINDEL: She was here—but her father caught her. Did you hear?

MANKE: How long ago was this?

HINDEL: A while. He's probably asleep himself now. She'll be down soon.

REIZEL: Come on, Manke, let's go out into the street, it's raining. And the drops are like pearls. The first shower of May. Who wants to come and take a bath?

MANKE: *(At the window:)* I didn't know it was raining. Looks inviting. I love the smell. Let's go out.

BASHA: At home when we have a shower like this the gutters run over and the streets flood, so we take off our shoes and stockings and dance barefoot in the rain. Let's take our shoes off!

MANKE: *(Taking off her stockings:)* Let's get soaked! They say standing in a May shower makes you grow.

BASHA: I'm going to splash you—. *(Takes her hair down)* I'm going to wash my hair—get it as drenched as leaves on the trees.

HINDEL: Wait. Wait. "Uncle" might not be asleep yet. What if he hears us.

(All listen.)

REIZEL: That's him, snoring. Let's go.

MANKE: Wait. Let me get Rifkele.

(BASHA and REIZEL go out. MANKE taps on the ceiling. outside sounds of the girls playing and shouting: "Come out! Come out!")

(RIFKELE, in her nightgown, appears from upstairs in the window.)

RIFKELE: Manke? Manke—did you call me?

(MANKE *takes a chair and places it under the window, she stands and reaches for* RIFKELE's *hand.*)

MANKE: I did. Come, we'll stand in the rain, splash water over each other and grow taller.

RIFKELE: Sh-sh. Not so loud. I snuck out of bed. So papa wouldn't hear. I'm scared he'll beat me.

MANKE: Don't be scared of your father. He's asleep. Come on. Let's go out into the rain. I'll put your hair down. *(She undoes* RIFKELE's *braids.)* There. I'll wash it in the rain. Like this.

RIFKELE: I only have a nightgown on. I laid in bed waiting for father to fall asleep. Then I heard you tapping. I snuck away, barefoot, so father wouldn't hear.

(MANKE *embraces* RIFKELE.)

MANKE: My Rifkele. I'll wash you in the rain. The night is beautiful, the rain is warm, and the air it smells so nice. Come.

RIFKELE: Sh-sh. Sh-sh. Father. He hit me. He locked the door. And hid the key under the Holy Scroll. I couldn't sleep. I heard you call me. You called me softly. And I couldn't help myself—I had to come. I stole the key from the Scroll. My heart was pounding in my chest. Pounding.

MANKE: Wait, I'll come to you. I'm coming to you. I'll be there in a second.

(HINDEL *who has been listening from her compartment, is excited, and talks to herself:*)

HINDEL: God help me get both of them—tonight. I'll take them right to Shloyme's. I'll just present her; "here you are. Here's your bread and your butter. Now rent a place and marry me and become as respectable as any other." *(Stops, looks up.)* Dear God, Father of us all.

Mother, in your grave, pray for me. Let my troubles come to an end. Let me have my own home! *(Pause)* If God is good to me, I'll have a Holy Scroll written in His honor. And every Sabbath I'll give three pounds of candles to the religious schools. *(Long pause as she thinks.)* God is good. God is good. Father in Heaven. Mother, pray for me. Don't be silent. Pray. Try your best for me. *(Begins to pack again)* I'll be ready. *(She closes her curtain. Long pause)*

(MANKE leads in RIFKELE, both are wet.)

MANKE: *(Softly:)* Sweetheart, are you cold? Come close to me. Closer. Warm yourself against me. Like that. Let's sit down on the sofa.

(MANKE and RIFKELE sit.)

MANKE: Like this. Rest your head against my breasts. There. Like that. Press against me. Feel the water? It's cool, like it's running between us. *(Pause)* Can I see your breasts? I want to wash them with the rainwater that's trickling down my arm. Your breasts are white and—soft. The blood in them cools under the touch—like white snow—or ice. They smell like the grass in the meadow. I let down your hair. *(Runs her fingers through RIFKELE's hair.)* And I held you like this and washed you in the rain. Your hair smells sweet. Like the rain. *(She buries her face in RIFKELE's hair.)* I smell the spring. Fresh air. Tall grass. An apple on a tree branch. Cool me, with your wet hair. *(Rubs her face in RIFKELE's hair.)* Cool me—like that. Wait. I want to comb you like a bride—two long black braids. *(As she does:)* Do you mind, Rifkele? Do you?

RIFKELE: No.

MANKE: You are the bride—what a beautiful bride. It's Sabbath eve and you are sitting with your papa and mama at the table. And I—am your sweetheart. Your

groom. And I've come as your guest. What do you say?
Do you like this game?

RIFKELE: I do.

MANKE: Wait. Now wait. Your father and mother have
gone to bed. The sweethearts are left alone at the table.
I'll bet we're bashful, don't you?

RIFKELE: Yes, Manke.

MANKE: Then—we move closer, after all we are bride
and groom, you and I. We embrace. *(She puts her arm
around* RIFKELE.*)* Tighter. And kiss—softly like this.
(Kisses RIFKELE.*)* And we blush—we're bashful. It's
nice, Rifkele, isn't it?

RIFKELE: Yes, Manke. Yes.

*(*MANKE *whispers in* RIFKELE's *ear.)*

MANKE: And then we go to bed together. No one sees,
no one hears. Only you and I. Do you want to sleep
with me tonight?

RIFKELE: I do. I do.

MANKE: Let's go. Come on.

RIFKELE: I'm scared of my father. If he wakes up—

MANKE: Wait. Let's wait, then. *(Thinks then:)* Maybe we
should get away from here. Then we'd be together all
day and all night. With no fathers, no mothers. No one
to yell at you, or beat you. Just me and you. For days
at a time. We could be so happy. What do you say,
Rifkele?

RIFKELE: Won't my father know?

MANKE: No. We'll run away tonight—with Hindel to
her new house. She has a house with Shloyme, she told
me. Things will be good there. Plenty of young people
there—army officers. And we'll be alone togther—all
day long. We can dress up as officers ourselves if you

like and go "horseback riding". Come on Rifkele, do you want to?

RIFKELE: And Papa won't hear?

MANKE: No, no. He won't hear. He's sound asleep. Listen—hear him snoring? *(Goes to* HINDEL's *compartment and opens the curtain.)* To your new place. Let's go. Take us away now.

HINDEL: Right, right. I'll take you to Shloyme. He'll find us a place now.

*(*HINDEL *throws a dress on* RIFKELE.)*

MANKE: *(Dressing* RIFKELE:*)* Wait until you see how nice everything will be. We'll have such fun.

(Dressed, grabbing what's at hand, they go, running into BASHA *and* REIZEL *at the door, both drenched.)*

REIZEL & BASHA: What's? Where are you going?

MANKE: Sh-sh. Quiet. We're going out for a beer—and a lemonade.

(They go.)

REIZEL: They're up to something, aren't they?

BASHA: They are.

REIZEL: Something—. Oh my God!

BASHA: What? Not that!

REIZEL: It's none of our business. Put out the lamp and get to bed. We know nothing.

(They turn down the wick in the lamp. The girls go to their "compartments".)

REIZEL: That fortune-teller was right. She's right.

(Silence)

(Stage is empty, then BASHA *runs out screaming.)*

REIZEL: What is it, Basha?

BASHA: I'm scared to sleep. I feel my mother's here—
with her thorns flying around my room.

REIZEL: The Holy Scroll in the room above has been
defiled. There's nothing to protect us now.

BASHA: Something bad's going to happen tonight. My
heart's racing.

*(From above: sounds of scraping of chairs, etc. Then footsteps
coming down the stairs.)*

YEKEL: *(Off:)* Rifkele! Rifkele! Where are you?

REIZEL: *(To BASHA:)* Lie down and pretend you're
sleeping. We know nothing.

*(YEKEL hurries in, holding a candle. over his nightclothes, he
has thrown on a coat.)*

YEKEL: Rifkele! Rifkele! Is Rifkele down here?

(No reply)

(YEKEL tears open the curtains.)

YEKEL: Rifkele! Where is she?

(YEKEL "wakes" BASHA and REIZEL.)

YEKEL: Where is Rifkele? Rifkele! Where is she?

(The girls pretend to have woken up.)

REIZEL & BASHA: What?? We don't know.

YEKEL: You don't know? You don't know? *(He hurries
upstairs.)*

(Pause)

*(Suddenly YEKEL stumbles back in, dragging SARAH by the
hair. Both in their nightclothes)*

YEKEL: Where is your daughter? Your daughter—
where is she?!!

(Girls huddle in terror. Quick curtain)

END OF ACT TWO

ACT THREE

(Same as ACT ONE)

(The room is in disarray. SARAH is picking things up. Early morning)

SARAH: Yekel! What's the matter with you Yekel? *(Goes to RIFKELE's door and looks inside:)* Why are you sitting in there? *(Continues to pick up)* This is a nightmare. Does he have to throw everything away? *(Back to the door:)* Yekel? Say something. What's wrong with you? *(Turns back)* What's he doing? Sitting in front of the Holy Scroll. What's he thinking about? What is there to think about? Go to the police, talk to the captain. Find the man who did this. There's still time. *(Back to the door:)* Say something! *(She sits and begins to cry.)* He sits there like a madman, staring at the Holy Scroll, mumbling. Doesn't he hear me? Doesn't he see me? What's possessed him? *(Stands, to YEKEL:)* What do I care—this place or another? You want me to go, I'll go. I won't starve. I know how to take care of myself. *(Packs, pause)*

(YEKEL enters from RIFKELE's room. He appears lost.)

YEKEL: I'll go. You'll go. Rifkele will go. Everything and everybody will go. *(Points to the cellar.)* Down there. It's God's will.

SARAH: Yekel, what's happened to you? Have you gone crazy? *(Approaches him)* Think about this. Something terrible has happened. I agree. We aren't the first people to have something terrible happen to them. Come on. Let's hunt out Shloyme. Offer him two, three hundred rubles to give us back our child. He'll do that. Sure. So—why have you been just sitting in there? What's wrong with you?

YEKEL: It's over. The devil owns my soul. Nothing can change that. Nothing. It's God's will.

SARAH: God's will? You talked yourself into that. It's your will I'm talking about. Do you love your daughter? Yekel? Yekel? What's come over you? And while there's still time. He might take her away while we're wasting time here. Let's find him. Hindel's taken her to him. Why are you just standing there? *(Suddenly:)* I've sent for Reb Ali. Maybe you will talk to him. *(Pause)* What are you staring at out there? *(Pause)* Say something! You'll drive me crazy! *(She cries.)*

YEKEL: No more home. No more wife. No more daughter. Down into the cellar. Back to the brothel. We don't need a daughter now. We don't need her. She's what her mother was. God's will. Back to the cellar. Down to the brothel.

SARAH: You want to go to the cellar? Go then. See if I care. *(Packs)* He wants to throw everything away. What's wrong with him? If you're going to just stand there like an idiot, I'll go myself then. *(Takes off her earrings)* I'll go over to Shloyme's and offer him my diamond earrings. *(Takes out a gold chain)* And if that's not enough, I'll throw in a hundred ruble note.

(SARAH searches YEKEL's pockets, he offers no resistance.)

SARAH: I'll be back with Rifkele. Shloyme will do that for me. *(Goes, slamming the door)*

YEKEL: *(Alone:)* It's over. The devil got her too. No more daughter. No more Holy Scroll. Down into the brothel with everything. Back to the brothel. God's will.

(Long pause)

(REIZEL *appears in the doorway.* YEKEL *looks at her.*)

REIZEL: I went for Reb Ali. Your wife sent me. He'll be here soon.

YEKEL: The devil has won her. It's over. It's too late. It's God's will.

REIZEL: She was such a nice girl. It's a pity.

(YEKEL *looks at* REIZEL.*)

REIZEL: Your wife told me to stay with you until she got back.

YEKEL: Don't be scared. I'm not mad yet. Not yet. God has punished me.

REIZEL: Who could have seen this coming? She was such an innocent girl. It's heartbreaking.

(REB ALI *hurries in with a lantern.*)

REB ALI: What's so important that you had to see me so early? It's almost time for morning prayers.

YEKEL: *(Not looking at* REB ALI*)* The Holy Scroll has been defiled, Reb Ali. Violated most foully.

REB ALI: What are you saying? God help us, the whole town will have to atone for this sin. What happened? Tell me, man! Dear God in Heaven.

YEKEL: Down into the brothel. *(Points, then to* REIZEL*)* Go, with the rest of them. Down into the brothel. No more Holy Scroll.

REB ALI: What are you saying? What happened here? Tell me!

REIZEL: No, Rebbi. Not the Holy Scroll. His daughter. Rifkele. The Holy Scroll has not been defiled. It's still in there. *(Points to* RIFKELE's *room)*

REB ALI: Thank God. But you are sure about this?

REIZEL: I am.

REB ALI: Thank God. I can breathe again. *(To* YEKEL*)* Why did you say that? *(To* REIZEL*)* Did his daughter go away? And she's not back? *(To* YEKEL*)* Who's looking for her?

YEKEL: My daughter is holier to me than a Holy Scroll.

REB ALI: Don't talk like that. Be quiet and don't make a scene. Who's looking for her? To bring her back. Anyone? Why are you just standing there? Why haven't you gone after her?

REIZEL: His wife went to get her.

REB ALI: Do they know where the girl went?

REIZEL: Yes. She'll bring her home soon.

REB ALI: So—then what's the problem? You want the whole town to know about this? Some things are best hidden. Some bad things. You want a possible father-in-law to hear about this? It'd cost you another two hundred in dowry.

YEKEL: It's over. Let them know. No more daughter. No more Holy Scroll. Into the cellar. Into the brothel with everything.

REB ALI: Stop it! Don't be stupid. So—a bad thing's happened. May Heaven watch over all of us. So? So what? Bad things happen to lots of people. The Lord sends help and things turn out just fine. The important thing is to keep it a secret. Hear nothing. See nothing. Just wash your hands clean of it and forget about it. *(To* REIZEL:*)* You—keep quiet about this. This doesn't leave this room. Do you hear me? *(To* YEKEL*)* I talked to her. *(Looks back at* REIZEL*)* We talked. And now we're finished.

*(*REIZEL *gets the hint and goes.)*

REB ALI: I spoke with the prospective groom's father. I spoke with him at the synagogue between afternoon

and evening prayers. He's almost ready to talk
business. Of course, I had to explain that the bride's
family wasn't well-placed in society. But I think
another hundred rubles will fix that. One's family
doesn't count for as much as it used to. With God's
help I'll bring him by this Sabbath. We'll have the
young man tested in his studies. So—no one should
hear about this—thing that's happened. It could spoil
everything. This father comes from a fine family and
the son has a good head on his shoulders. So there.
Relax. Trust in the Lord and all will turn out for the
best. With God's help I am going home to prepare for
the morning prayer. As soon as the girl returns, let me
know. Don't forget. *(Starts to go)*

YEKEL: Listen to me, Rebbi. Take your Holy Scroll. I
don't need it now.

REB ALI: What are you talking about? What's gotten
into you? Are you stark raving mad?

YEKEL: My daughter has gone to a brothel. The Scroll
has been desecrated. God has punished me.

REB ALI: What are you raving about?

YEKEL: I am a wretched sinner. I know that too well.
But why couldn't he have broken the feet I walk on—
or taken my life in its prime? Why did He want my
daughter? My poor, blameless daughter.

REB ALI: Listen to me. Don't talk like that against the
Lord.

YEKEL: And why not? What's to stop me. It's the truth.
I am Yekel Tschaftchovitch. The "Uncle" of a brothel. I
say this—even to God. I'm no longer afraid. I went to
you, I told you everything. You advised me to have a
Holy Scroll written. In there, I placed it—in her room.
I stood before it night after night, and said: 'You are a
true God. You know everything. You will punish me.

Fine. Punish me. Punish my wife. We have sinned. But
my little innocent daughter. Protect her. Have pity on
her.

REB ALI: But what bad has happened to her? She'll
return. She'll still make a fine pious Jewish wife.

YEKEL: Forget it. The devil won her. She'll be pulled
down. Once she begins, she'll not stop. If not today,
tomorrow—the devil has won her soul. I know. I know
too well.

REB ALI: Nonsense. Get ahold of yourself. Pray hard for
God's forgiveness. Give up this business of yours. With
God's help your daughter will get married—just like
all Jewish women, and bring you years of happiness.

YEKEL: Too late, Rebbi. Too late. If only she had
died when she was still a child, I'd have nothing to
complain about. I'd know she was dead—that I'd
buried an innocent creature. I'd visit her grave and tell
myself, "Here lies your child. You may be a sinner,
but here lies your innocent child, your dear daughter."
But instead, what am I left with? I'm a sinner. I leave
behind a sinner. And so from generation to generation
passes sin.

REB ALI: Don't talk like that. A Jew does not say such
things. Trust in the Lord and say, "The past is dead
and buried".

YEKEL: *(Interrupting:)* Don't try to console me, Rebbi.
It's too late for that. Like a hangman's rope, sin
encircles me and mine. God's will. But why, Rebbi
should He will this? What harm could it have done to
allow me, Yekel Tschaftchovitch, to climb up out of
the shit? *(He goes to* RIFKELE's *room and brings out the
Holy Scroll. Holds it up:)* You are a great God. Because
you are our Lord. I, Yekel Tchaftchovitch, have sinned.
(Beats his breast) My sins. My sins. I ask for a miracle.
Send down a pillar of fire and consume me. Here,

where I stand. Open up the earth and swallow me. But save my child. Send her back to me as pure and as innocent as when she left. I know—you can do this. For You everything is possible. Give me a miracle. You are almighty God. But if You don't—then You are no God of mine. And I, Yekel Tchaftschovitch, tell you that you are as vengeful as any common man.

(REB ALI *grabs the Holy Scroll from* YEKEL.)

REB ALI: You are talking to God! (*Takes the Scroll back to* RIFKELE's *room.*) Beg Him to forgive you.

YEKEL: I'm only telling him the truth. (*He follows* REB ALI *into* RIFKELE's *room.*) If he's really God, give me my miracle!

(REB ALI *and* YEKEL *are gone.*)

(SARAH *runs in, fixes her hair and calls:*)

SARAH: Shloyme, come in! Why are you staying outside?

SHLOYME: (*Off*) Where's Yekel? Let him know I'm— (*He enters.*) —doing what I can. People like us—Yekel and me—need to stick together. No matter how he talks to me.

(SARAH *locks* RIFKELE's *door, locking in* REB ALI *and* YEKEL.)

SARAH: Let him stay in there. (*She smiles.*) These last few days he's turned into a real saint. Seeks out only pious Jews for company. (*Locks the main door*) And your "bride"? She doesn't give up does she? She's not an easy one to get rid of, is she? She's probably sniffing out your trail as we speak. (*Smiles*) Shloyme. Shloyme—you can do better than that thing. (*Opens a window*) So dark in here, like we're in mourning.

SHLOYME: I've said I'd help out, so I'm here. As a favor to you. Even if you haven't been too nice to me lately. But I forget that. As for Hindel, she's useful.

SARAH: To a young man like you? What can you see in a whore like her? She looks like a scarecrow. What do you know about her? You know she's gone from brothel to brothel. You are young! And now—you're getting some money. What do you need her for? With a couple hundred rubles in your pocket—you'll see—there are other—better—girls to choose. Why not? You're young and handsome, aren't you? *(Slaps him on the back.)* Listen to me. I've never been mean to you, though maybe lately I haven't treated you as well as I should. But I've always been Sarah to you, haven't I?

SHLOYME: Why are you saying this? You think I'm serious about that girl. She was good for a few rubles, that's all. You think I'd marry—that? My mother would curse every bone in my body. I have a respectable mother. And sister.

SARAH: So you must have all sorts of better business prospects than tying yourself down to that horror and opening a place with her. Business is good now, by the way. A whore like that just pulls you down.

(SARAH hands SHLOYME her earrings.)

SARAH: Here, take these and here's another hundred rubles. Now tell me where Rifkele is.

SHLOYME: What you say is true. I'll bet you were a good whore. *(Winks at her)* Though lately you've been full of yourself. Never forget—who we are.

SARAH: So tell me, Shloyme, where is she? Tell me the truth. Don't worry that I'm her mother; you can't shock me. Have you taken her to a—?

SHLOYME: She's nearby. If I tell you I can bring her here—then I can bring her. Let me tell you—she's a prize. Those eyes. The way she moves. And she knows what to do.

SARAH: Yes. Like mother like daughter. Now tell me, Shloyme, where are you keeping her? You can tell me. *(Coquettishly:)* You young, handsome man, tell me.

SHLOYME: It's not far. Not far at all.

HINDEL: *(Off, banging on the door:)* Get away from her! Get away from that woman!

SARAH: Let her bang her head against the door. She doesn't give up, does she? How 'dare' he leave you for one second! *(Flirting with him:)* Shame on you for wasting your time with trash like that. What do you need her for? You want a girl. I'll get you one. A beauty. You'll see. *(Winks at him)*

(HINDEL forces open the door and enters.)

HINDEL: What are you doing to him? Go to hell. Their daughter ran away— *(Taking SHLOYME by the hand)* He doesn't know where she is. What do they want from you?

SARAH: So this is your "taste" in women? That thing? Don't make me laugh. *(She laughs.)*

HINDEL: She's crazy. *(To SHLOYME)* You know nothing about Rifkele. *(Whispers:)* Let's go to Lodz now. We'll marry there. Rent a house— With two girls like we've got… Think what you're doing. *(Out loud:)* What do they want with you? You know nothing about her. Come on, Shloyme.

SARAH: Go, Shloyme, go with her. She's come to get you. To take you to Lodz. To get married. To set up house.

(SARAH laughs and takes SHLOYME away from HINDEL.)

SARAH: A young man, with a respectable mother—and your father, a pious Jew. What do you want with her? What does she want from you?

SHLOYME: Let's go, Sarah. We'll get Rifkele.

HINDEL: Don't tell her! You know nothing! *(Tries to block the door)* I won't let you out. Shloyme, it worked for them. Why not for us? Please, Shloyme, let's leave this place. We'll open our own business—you'll be rich!

SHLOYME: You just say the same thing over and over and over! *(Pushes her away)* I'll talk to you later. I'm busy now.

(SHLOYME goes out with SARAH, HINDEL follows.)

(SARAH runs back in and opens RIFKELE's door and calls:)

SARAH: Rifkele's coming home!

HINDEL: *(To SHLOYME:)* Don't tell her. I won't let you!

SHLOYME: Sarah, let's go.

SARAH: I'm coming, Shloyme.

(They are gone.)

(REB ALI enters with YEKEL.)

REB ALI: Praise the Lord. Praise be to the Heavenly Father. What did I tell you, see how the Almighty helps us. He punishes—yes. But he gives us the medicine as well as the disease. You have sinned, you have blasphemed which you must never do again. You must be reverent. Know what a Holy Scroll means and how a learned Jew acts. You'll go to the synagogue and make a generous donation. You'll fast and the Lord will forgive you.

(REB ALI looks at the distracted YEKEL.)

REB ALI: Have you heard what I said? With the help of the Almighty it will all turn out for the best. I'll go at once to the groom's father. We'll go over the details. Don't haggle. What's a hundred rubles, more or less. Remember who you are and who he is. Get it over quick, no idle chit-chat before—God forbid— something else happens. We have no time to waste. Are you listening to me? I'm talking to you!

YEKEL: *(As if to himself:)* I want to ask her one thing. Just one. But she has to tell me the truth—the whole truth. Yes or no.

REB ALI: Don't sin, man. Thank God that He has helped you.

YEKEL: I'll not lay a finger on her. Just the truth. Yes or no.

REB ALI: The truth. The truth. Heaven will help you. Everything will turn out for the best. I'm going to the young man's father. We were to meet at the synagogue—he must be waiting. *(Looks around)* Tell your wife, to clean up. And you—draw up the contract—quick before he hears anything about this. Set a date and have the bride go at once to meet her in-laws. No chit-chat, remember. The less said—the better, and the less he'll know. *(Starts to go)* Forget about all this nonsense. Trust in the Lord and rejoice in His comfort. And tell your wife to clean up. *(He goes.)*

YEKEL: *(Alone)* Just the truth. The simple truth. *(Silence)*

SARAH: *(Entering:)* Come in. Come in. Your father won't beat you. *(Pause)* Go in. Get in.

(SARAH pushes RIFKELE into the room.)

SARAH: Are you just going to stand there? A lot of thanks we get—for all our trouble in bringing you up. We'll talk about that later. Go to your room. Comb your hair. Put on a dress. We're expecting guests! *(To YEKEL)* I just spoke with Reb Ali. He's going to get the groom's father. Look at this place. It's a mess. *(She starts to straighten up.)*

*(*YEKEL *looks at* RIFKELE, *approaches her, takes her gently by the hand and leads her to the table.)*

YEKEL: Don't be scared. I won't hurt you. *(He sits down.)* Here, sit beside me. Sit down.

RIFKELE: I'd rather stand.

YEKEL: Sit down.

*(*YEKEL *seats* RIFKELE.*)*

YEKEL: Don't be scared.

RIFKELE: Why should I be scared?

YEKEL: Rifkele, talk to me, Rifkele. You are my daughter. I am your father. She is your mother. Tell me, daughter. Tell me the truth. Don't be scared of me. No need to be ashamed in front of me. All this—is not because of your sins. Not yours. But mine. And your mother's. Because of our sins. Tell me, daughter—

SARAH: Talk about this later. What do you want her to say? She just got back. Let her get dressed, company's coming.

YEKEL: Let go of her!

SARAH: You're acting crazy today. What's wrong with you?

YEKEL: *(To* RIFKELE:*)* I won't beat you. *(Puts his fingers around her neck)* If only I had wrung your neck before you ever grew up, that would have been better —for you and me. But don't be scared. I won't harm you. It's not your sins God is punishing, it's ours. I watched over you like the apple of my eye. I had a Holy Scroll written for you. I placed it in your room and prayed to it night and day. "Protect her from evil. Punish me. And her. But spare my daughter." You'd grow up and I'd find a good husband for you. He'd be respectable.

You'd live with me here, both of you, I'd pay for everything. You'd both...

RIFKELE: Why do I have to get married now? There's plenty of time for that: I'm not that old.

SARAH: Don't argue with your father.

RIFKELE: You're trying to turn me into a Rabbi's wife. Mama wasn't married at my age.

SARAH: Stop it or I'll slap your face. She's gone one night and listen how she talks.

RIFKELE: In one night I learned a lot.

YEKEL: Leave her alone! I want to ask her one thing. One thing only. Tell me the truth. I won't beat you. I won't lay a finger on you. I won't blame you. Tell me— tell me—the—truth. The—

SARAH: What are you asking her? What do you want from her?

YEKEL: I'm not talking to you. Don't be ashamed in front of me. I'm your father. You can tell me everything. Speak openly. Are you—are you still as pure as when you left this house. Are you still a virgin? *(Shouts)* Are you still a virgin?!!

SARAH: Leave her alone. She's done nothing wrong. Let her go.

YEKEL: Just tell me the truth. I'll believe you. Look me in the eye. Are you a virgin? Look me in the eye! Look at me!

(RIFKELE hides her face with her a shawl.)

SARAH: Why are you hiding your face? Take that away. We're inside, you don't need that.

YEKEL: Tell me now. Don't be ashamed. I won't harm you. Are you still a chaste Jewish daughter? Tell me! Are you a virgin?!

RIFKELE: *(Trying to hide her face:)* I don't know.

YEKEL: You don't know? You don't know? Then
who does know? What does that mean— "you don't
know"? The truth! Now. Are you still—.

RIFKELE: It was all right for Mama. It was all right for
you! I know everything about you! Beat me! Beat me! I
dare you!

*(SARAH goes to hit RIFKELE, YEKEL pushes her aside.
RIFKELE cries.)*

(Pause)

*(SARAH continues to clean up, then goes to RIFKELE, helps
her up and leads her off to her room. SARAH returns.)*

SARAH: Yekel, think what you're doing, for God's sake.
Who needs to know anything? *(Pause)* Calm down.
(Pause) Rifkele will get married and we'll live to see her
make us happy.

(YEKEL is silent.)

SARAH: Put on your coat, they'll be here soon. Who
needs to know anything?

(YEKEL stares into space.)

(SARAH brings him his coat and hat.)

SARAH: What a terrible thing. Who could have seen
it coming? *(She goes off to RIFKELE's room and returns.)*
We'll talk about all this later. Terrible. You bring up
children with so much care and worry and then…

(Footsteps)

SARAH: They're here. For the love of God, Yekel,
remember we can fix everything.

*(REB ALI and a STRANGER enter. SARAH goes to welcome
them.)*

REB ALI: Good morning.

SARAH: Good morning. Welcome.

(SARAH *offers chairs to* REB ALI *and the* STRANGER.)

REB ALI: And where is the father of the bride?

SARAH: Come and join them, Yekel.

(YEKEL *joins them.*)

REB ALI: Let's get right down to business. *(Points to* YEKEL*)* This gentleman wishes to bring your two families together. He has a fine daughter and wants for her husband a scholar well versed in Rabbinical Law. He'll support the couple for life.

STRANGER: I'm interested.

YEKEL: Yes, my friend. A virtuous Jewish daughter. A model child.

REB ALI: He's agreed to a dowry of five hundred rubles—cash. To be paid at the time of the engagement. And he'll support the couple for life. He will treat your son as his own.

STRANGER: I won't waste my breath boosting of the value of my goods. In two more years of study, he'll have it all at his fingertips.

REB ALI: Of course. Of course. This gentleman will take care of him like the apple of his eye. He'll have the best of everything here. He'll be able to sit and study to his heart's content.

YEKEL: *(Pointing to* RIFKELE's *room:)* Yes, he'll sit in there and study the sacred book. I have a virginal Jewish daughter.

(YEKEL *goes and drags* RIFKELE *out. She is only half dressed.*)

YEKEL: Your son will marry this pure Jewish daughter. She will bear him pure Jewish children—as a pious daughter would. *(To* SARAH*)* Isn't that so? *(He starts*

to laugh, then to the STRANGER:*)* Yes, my friend—she'll
make a pure, pious little whore. My wife will lead
her under the wedding canopy. Down you go. Down
below. Down. Into the brothel.

*(*YEKEL *drags* RIFKELE *to the door.)*

YEKEL: Whore! Whore!

SARAH: You're mad! You're mad!

*(*SARAH *tries to take* RIFKELE *from* YEKEL, *he pushes her
aside and drags his daughter out by the hair.)*

YEKEL: Down into the brothel, you whore!!

(They are gone.)

STRANGER: What is this?

*(*REB ALI *leads the* STRANGER *out.)*

(Pause)

*(*YEKEL *returns with* REB ALI.*)*

YEKEL: And take your Holy Scroll with you! I don't
need it anymore!

(Curtain)

END OF PLAY

CPSIA information can be obtained
at www.ICGtesting.com
Printed in the USA
LVHW081436110122
708132LV00017B/1436